*How to Choose and Use the
Right Therapist for You*

How to Choose
and Use
the Right
Therapist
for You

Jean and Jim Erwin

SHEED ANDREWS AND McMEEL, Inc.
Subsidiary of Universal Press Syndicate
KANSAS CITY

Library of Congress Cataloging in Publication Data

Erwin, Jean.
  How to choose and use the right therapist for you.

  An outgrowth of a project sponsored by the Mental Health
Association of Johnson County, Kansas
  Bibliography: p.
  1. Psychotherapists—Evaluation. 2. Psychotherapy—
Evaluation. 3. Consumer education. I. Erwin, Jim,
joint author. II. Mental Health Association of Johnson
County, Kansas. III. Title.
RC480.5.E78   616.8'91   78-17129
ISBN 0-8362-2601-1

*All royalties from the sale of this book will go to the Mental
Health Association of Johnson County, Kansas, a nonprofit
organization.*

CONTENTS

ACKNOWLEDGMENTS

To begin at the beginning: In the spring of 1975 a practicing psychotherapist talked to a local group called Breakthrough about the accountability of psychotherapists to their clients/patients. Breakthrough is sponsored by the Mental Health Association of Johnson County, Kansas. Its membership is made up of people who are or have been in therapy, members of their families, and individuals concerned about mental health—their own as well as others. So their interest in the subject was considerably more than academic. So much so, in fact, that as an outgrowth of the program, several members of the group decided to put together a modest brochure called *How to Choose a Therapist.*

From that point on, the concept grew broader in scope and involved many more people. In the spring of 1976 the project was presented to the Board of the Mental Health Association of Johnson County and to the Association's professional consultants. Both groups gave the project their approval and—most important—their continuing support. Without their help and encouragement throughout the more than eighteen months between inception and publication, it is unlikely the project could have been completed.

A General Therapy Guide Committee was formed with a large and flexible membership. All were volunteers. Professionals and nonprofessionals alike served on the committee at various times and attended meetings. From the larger group there came a smaller one called the Core Committee, a decision-making body made up of a cross-section of professionals (social workers, psychologists, and psychiatrists) and lay people. The way in which this group pushed the project through to completion is unique in our experience.

A table of contents was developed and people from both within and outside the committee agreed to prepare material for various chapters. When the material was received, it was submitted to Breakthrough and the General Committee for discussion and processing. The material was then returned to the Core Committee for further processing, after which it was turned over to the writers (Jean and Jim Erwin). It was our function to take the material which had originated with many different people and synthesize it into a coherent whole. When the writing was completed, the material was sent back to the Core Committee, where it was either accepted or returned to the writers with further recommendations.

All of the material in this book went through the process described above and was approved by the Core Committee, people representing both the private sector and public sector and different disciplines—a unique blend of psychotherapists in private practice, Community Mental Health Center personnel, and members of the Mental Health Association, both lay and professional. This kind of project in which the professional and the nonprofessional generated ideas and exchanged them, and agreed on the result, was a milestone in itself.

To acknowledge by name everyone who has worked on the project is obviously impossible, but we do want to express our special appreciation to those most intimately involved. We have omitted any reference to professional titles, degrees, or affiliations so as to reflect the equal importance of both lay and professional contributions.

Our particular thanks to Betty Barker-Smith who chaired the Core Committee, for bringing to that task an openness and a deep commitment to group process that facilitated the work of the committee and each individual member immeasurably. The other members of the Core Committee, in addition to the writers, were Hal Boyts, Janice Dobies, Hattie Jo Finney, Gordon McAfee, Beverly Rose, Barbara Routh, and Linda Varian Urda.

Our thanks, too, to the following individuals: Suzie Aron, Denis Carville, Carol Charismas, Louis Forman, Sharon L. Jacobs, Marjorie Kirkwood, Mary K. McNeive, Jean Dooley Peterson, Phillip Rosenshield, Marshall Saper, Mary Kay Smith, and Othello Dale Smith.

Acknowledgments

Our thanks to these organizations for their help and support: Breakthrough, the Johnson County Library, the Professional Consultants and the Board of the Mental Health Association of Johnson County, and Phi Gamma Delta Sorority.

Finally, our thanks to Jim Andrews, Donna Martin, and Tom Thornton of Sheed Andrews and McMeel, Inc., for their help in so many ways.

We would like to make a special acknowledgment to Public Citizen's Health Research Group in Washington, D.C., for generously allowing us to quote from their publication *Through The Mental Health Maze* (© 1975, Public Citizen's Health Research Group). Where we have done so, the quotation is followed by a page reference to their book. Although our emphasis, approach and scope are often quite different from theirs, we do share a common belief in both the client/patient's ability and responsibility "to choose and use the right therapist" and the considerations that go into making that choice.

JEAN AND JIM ERWIN
*for the Mental Health Association
of Johnson County, Kansas*

INTRODUCTION

Most people going into therapy have little or no idea of how to choose a therapist. In fact, the concept of "choosing" or "shopping for" a therapist may in itself appear to be an odd one. After all, aren't *all* psychotherapists equally competent to deal with all kinds of clients/patients and with all kinds of problems? And isn't the person with emotional problems at least partly disqualified by those problems from making the wisest choice as to who can best help in dealing with them?

The answer to the first question is, "No, they are not. If they were, there would be no need for a book like this—a need first pointed out to the group responsible for its beginnings by a psychotherapist himself."

The answer to the second question—whether emotional problems affect one's ability to choose a therapist—is a little more complicated and will be dealt with in detail later on. It can best be answered here by the phrase, "Not nearly as much as the question itself implies." One of the most important things for a person considering therapy to know—possibly *the* most important thing—is that the greatest contribution to be made in working through his/her problems will be made by himself/herself. And the earlier in the therapy process this contribution begins, the better. What better place for it to begin, then, than in the choice of the therapist?

All well and good—but what standards should be used, what questions asked, how large a part (and what kind) should gut feelings play in the selection process? In other words, the potential client/patient may ask, what are the elements I should consider to increase my chances of making the best decision in choosing a therapist? And once that choice is made, what can I do to make my therapy as effective as possible?

The answer to those questions is what this book is all about.

Just look at the Contents. Most of the chapters are purposely laid out in question form: Do I Need Therapy? What Is Available? What Can I Expect? How Can I Make Therapy an Investment with Positive Returns? What Do I Do if I Feel Stuck? What Do I Do when I Am Finished?

Simple, important questions. And with them what we hope you will see as straightforward though not always simple answers. Answers as free of unnecessary technical jargon as we have been able to make them.

This book is the work of many minds, many hands, and many hearts. It involves the best efforts of professionals—psychotherapists of many different orientations—past and present clients/patients, and interested lay people.

So the "we" above is not the usual anonymous editorial "we." It is the people who have shared their experiences, their skills, and their pain so that you might be able to find here at least some of the things you need to make your therapy as successful as possible.

We offer it with hope, with a sense of excitement at what it may mean to you, and—most of all—with love.

1

Do I Need Therapy?
(Do Those I Love Need Therapy?)

Something triggers the question.

It may happen quickly, dramatically—or it may develop gradually over a long period of time. There may be warning signals or symptoms to make you aware that something is wrong or you may be receiving complaints from other people which cause you to suspect that a problem exists.

You may feel certain that you need professional help or you may be unsure and want an evaluation to see whether therapy is advised. Or possibly your concern is not for yourself but for someone close to you, someone you love. But the fact that the question is asked in itself indicates that there may be a problem.

What follows is not intended to be a comprehensive listing of all symptoms, but some examples we hope will help you resolve the question.

EMOTIONAL SYMPTOMS

You may have feelings of "just not functioning up to par"—feelings that are vaguely disturbing and last a long time but somehow don't seem serious enough to warrant seeking help. *Loss of energy, loss of enthusiasm, loss of interest* are all "early warning signs" that deserve attention.

Emotional problems of a less severe nature can be more disabling in the long run simply because you may never experience them strongly enough to seek help.

Your problems may be much more severe. You may feel *unable to concentrate, unable to make decisions, unable to cope* any longer and simply *stop functioning.* You may experience *severe sadness, fearfulness,* or *anxiety* for no apparent reason. You may feel an acute *loss of self-esteem and self-confidence.* You may find yourself *withdrawing from people, avoiding social contact.* You may be *unable to experience or express anger in an appropriate, nondestructive way* or you may experience *wide mood swings*—and you may be frightened by these feelings or apparent lack of feelings.

It is not unusual to experience feelings or symptoms like these. Anyone can experience some of them during a lifetime. But when more than one of them occurs at the same time or the feelings are severe—or both—it is best to consider seeking professional help with your problems.

It is also possible that you are a person who has *never been able to cope, to function comfortably,* and whose lifelong patterns reflect this inability. In other words, you *have not learned the coping skills necessary to function effectively and well.* Often therapy consists of learning these skills, and there is good reason to believe that therapy could be helpful to you.

PHYSICAL/PSYCHOSOMATIC SYMPTOMS

Your symptoms or warning signals may be physical, the kind produced by chronic stress: *recurrent headaches, muscle pain, backaches, rapid heartbeats, severe loss of appetite* and *inability to eat, constipation, sleeping problems, hyperventilation (excessively rapid and deep breathing),* and *gastrointestinal troubles,* such as *diarrhea, ulcers,* and *colitis.*
Symptoms like these could be physical or psychosomatic or both. In any case, if you have physical symptoms your first step should be to consult a doctor to investigate possible physical causes. However, if your doctor is unable to find a physical cause for your discomfort, you may want to consult a psychotherapist for an evaluation, since any kind of physical discomfort may have an emotional cause.

SYMPTOMS INVOLVING RELATIONSHIPS

Your problems may involve relationships with others—your spouse, other members of your family, people you work with, your friends, or your neighbors. You may experience problems in this area such as an *inability to form relationships, frequent quarreling*

5

and bickering with others, nursing and carrying grudges, or a *deep-seated fear of other people.*

Where the problems involve family relationships, the person in the family who is feeling the most pain is not necessarily the one who needs most to be in therapy. In this kind of situation, it may be necessary for other family members to enter into therapy as well.

If you are married, you may find that you function well outside your marriage but are not satisfied with the relationship with your spouse. Or your spouse may feel this way.

One of the marriage partners may go into therapy for himself/herself and as a result make changes that alter the marital relationship—upset the balance. The other partner may need some therapy—or need to participate in the spouse's therapy—to keep up with the process.

SEXUAL PROBLEMS

Problems in the sexual area may be experienced in a number of ways: for example, by a man as *impotence,* by a woman as being *nonorgasmic,* by either or both as *general sexual dissatisfaction.* To put it simply, if you are not happy with your sex life, you may want to seek professional help.

6

HABIT PATTERNS

You may notice a habit pattern that acts as a warning signal. *Excessive drinking* and *drug abuse* are examples. Another is the *inability to follow through,* reflected in such things as changing jobs frequently. You may find yourself *constantly putting things off,* or you may be very *inflexible.*

UNEXPECTED REACTIONS TO CHANGE

Your feelings of needing help may be triggered by the unexpected way you react to a specific situation, a sudden surprise that you are not geared to deal with—such as a *job change* or *job loss,* the *death* of someone close to you, *moving, illness, childbirth and/or caring for babies* or *divorce.* And you can experience *stress with "good" changes as well as "bad" ones* if they occur suddenly or happen close together, because change of any kind is stressful.

Severe physical illness may have accompanying emotional problems. For example, patients who have had strokes, those with heart conditions, people with cancer, persons who have suffered the loss of body organs or parts, all may experience emotional problems as well as physical problems and require treatment in both areas. The post-partum depression sometimes experienced by women following childbirth may be severe enough to require help.

7

GOAL OR VALUE CLARIFICATION

Many people go into therapy who function well, don't really feel ill, but want to clarify their goals or are looking for personal growth and change and a greater sense of fulfillment in their lives. They may feel stuck, not getting on in life, just spinning their wheels—or they may be coping but feel that the price they are paying to cope is too high. They want to change, but change is frightening. Therapy provides a way to gain emotional support while changing and growing.

For example, many women today are involved in exploring new alternatives for themselves as they struggle to gain identity. And there are couples who may not be unhappy in their marriage relationship but are seeking to improve and enhance the relationship and see therapy as a way to accomplish this.

Some people who have had successful therapy in the past may go back to deal with new issues, because therapy can be a growth process as well as a healing process.

UNFINISHED BUSINESS

Sometimes people—and you may be one—have difficulty letting go of past events and relationships and are unable to enjoy what is available to them in the present. We can say that they don't live in the "here and now." Therapy would probably be very useful in dealing with this kind of problem.

COMPLAINTS FROM OTHERS

Up to this point we've dealt with problems or warning signs of which you are personally aware. But sometimes people are not aware that a problem exists and it falls to others to bring it to their attention. For example, when experiencing emotional distress, an individual is often unaware that what he/she needs is psychotherapy. In such a situation, family members may need to initiate contact with a therapist themselves—and even if the individual involved won't go, the others in the family can gain help by going themselves and finding out what to do.

If your receive feedback from others—family, friends, your physician, etc.—in the form of repeated complaints or concern about your behavior, it may well be that you are experiencing problems you're unaware of and need to seek professional help.

SYMPTOMS IN CHILDREN AND ADOLESCENTS

What kind of symptoms are likely to indicate problems in children and adolescents?

SCHOOL PROBLEMS:
The child who *consistently performs below his/her ability*

level may have a problem that requires professional help.

The whole area of developmental disabilities—physical or mental deficiencies—in children is often first noted in school. Some examples of these deficiencies would include *retardation, perceptual difficulties,* and *learning disabilities,* as well as *deficiencies in speech, eyesight, or hearing.* Emotional problems often go hand in hand with these disabilities and may require psychotherapy for the child and/or the family.

Repeated truancy is an indication of a child's problem. A child who experiences *frequent stomach aches* when it's time to go to school or is often "too sick" to go to classes may have problems requiring help.

PEER PROBLEMS:

All children experience some difficulties in relationships with other children their age from time to time, but repeated, frequent, or chronic problems in this area may be a warning that the child has a more serious problem. Some examples are *severe loneliness, bullying* others or *being bullied* by them, as well as being made a *scapegoat* by other children.

PROBLEM BEHAVIOR AT HOME:

Several examples are: *running away, temper tantrums,* and *withdrawal from contact and communication.*

10

EATING PROBLEMS:

Children's problems are often reflected in their eating habits such as the *compulsive eater* or the child who suffers from *severe loss of appetite.*

DRUG AND/OR ALCOHOL ABUSE:

"Trying" drugs and/or alcohol once or twice is not necessarily an indication of serious problems in a child or young adolescent, but *repeated experimenting* may be a signal for help.

PROBLEMS OF THE ELDERLY

Behavior which we would consider a warning signal if we observed it in a younger person is often attributed to senility when we see it in an elderly person—with the assumption that nothing can be done to help. Some examples are: *loss of memory, confusion, violent temper outbursts, depression, agitation,* and *bizarre behavior.*

If we make only one point regarding problems of the elderly, let it be this: Don't assume that the symptoms you see in an elderly person are solely due to senility; do seek an evaluation from a qualified professional to see if something can be done to help.

UNSURE? ASK FOR AN EVALUATION

If you are in doubt about whether therapy would

be useful in resolving your problems or those of someone close to you, ask the therapist you contact for an evaluation. After a few sessions the therapist should know whether therapy would be helpful. If the therapist thinks it would be useful but does not think he or she can help, ask for a referral to another therapist.

2

What Is Available?

Once you have decided that ongoing therapy may be what you need—or that at least you want to ask the advice of a therapist—the next question is, "How do I find help?" This chapter is designed to answer that question by suggesting a procedure to follow in looking for help and by listing some of the available sources of help.

It's a difficult chapter to write. First of all, it's difficult to suggest what you might do without knowing the very specific needs you or a loved one have. Secondly, there are often many mental health resources available in most metropolitan areas while there may be few or none in many small communities and in rural areas.

If we could give you a simple answer to the question, "How do I find help?" we would. In some cases, especially in emergency situations, the decision regarding what to do and where to turn may be reached quickly. (See Chapter 12 on emergencies.) But in most cases some time—possibly days or weeks—passes while you actively seek information and follow through on a decision to get help. So don't be discouraged if the first contact you make doesn't provide you with helpful information. Keep making contacts until you get what you want.

WHERE TO BEGIN

Many people first turn for help to their clergyman (priest, minister, rabbi), their medical doctor, lawyer, or school counselor. Each of these professionals may be able to help you or may refer you to a therapist, agency, or information source.

You may want to ask a neighbor, friend, coworker, or relative if he or she knows of someone— professional or lay person—whom you might call or the name of an agency where help might be available.

It's important to remember, though, that friends, neighbors, physicians, and clergy often are not familiar with the whole range of mental health services and therapists available in the community, and they may not know the competence of the therapist to whom you are being referred.

Keep in mind that you are not obligated to accept a referral from anyone. The person who was the right source of help for a neighbor or friend may not be the right source of help for you.

PUBLIC SOURCES OF INFORMATION

You may want to supplement or replace personal

16

contacts with public sources of information—such sources as community referral services or your local mental health association. These agencies can't provide direct services to you but they can provide information about what help is available. Public agencies like community mental health centers and private not-for-profit agencies such as those which offer family and children's services (both secular and religious) can provide services as well as referrals.

Other sources of information are the directories, registers, and similar publications put out by various agencies and professional groups. The *National Registry of Health Care Providers in Clinical Social Work* contains the names of social workers who have met specific educational requirements, including a core of clinical course work, and whose work has been reviewed by a local clinical peer review and standards committee (or some equivalent procedure). The *NASW Register of Clinical Social Workers* has similar requirements except that it does not require the core of clinical course work. Listing in the *National Register of Health Care Service Providers in Psychology* requires state licensing or certification and agreement by a team of reviewers that the psychologist's work experience involves "delivery of direct, preventive, assessment, and therapeutic intervention services to individuals" (*APA Monitor* as quoted in *Through the Mental Health Maze,* p. 23; hereafter cited as *Maze,* p. 23). Listing in the

17

register is voluntary. The *Biographical Directory of the American Psychiatric Association* lists its members geographically and notes those who have been certified by the American Board of Psychiatry and Neurology. Two other publications which list psychiatrists are the *American Medical Directory,* a three-volume set which lists every M.D. licensed to practice in the United States, and the *Directory of Medical Specialists.* In addition to these national publications, many communities have local directories. Local medical societies usually publish directories. Other professional societies— those for psychologists and social workers—often put out local directories, too. Sometimes state agencies which license or certify mental health professionals publish directories. Local community directories may also have listings of agencies and other resources. Some communities have these directories in their local public libraries. If your library doesn't have such a service, you may want to encourage library personnel to provide it. Local medical societies and other professional societies may also provide access to directories. University libraries are another possible place in which to find some of the directories discussed here.

You may decide to consult the Yellow Pages of your telephone book for information. A note of caution in this regard: there is no screening process required for such listings and the listings are often incomplete.

18

CHOICES AND QUALIFICATIONS

Therapists work in private practice and/or public agencies, private not-for-profit agencies, and hospitals.

A private practice (individual and/or group) is one operated for profit within the framework of the private free enterprise system.

A private not-for-profit agency is basically financed by private funds (such as United Way, foundation grants, endowments, etc.) and client/patient fees. This kind of agency serves the general public and usually charges fees based on a person's ability to pay.

A public agency is primarily funded by tax monies and client/patient fees. It must serve all individuals—regardless of their ability to pay—within a geographic area determined by the government unit which supplies the funds.

If you have a preference between a private therapist and an agency, be sure to tell your referring source. Regardless of which you choose, you will want to check out and assess the therapist's qualifications and training.

Qualifications and training *do not insure* a good match between you and a therapist, since there is more involved in a good match than qualifications and training alone. However, credentials *do insure* that a minimum amount of training and experience are

19

present. (See Chapter 3 for a description of the training and certification or licensing requirements for various kinds of therapists.)

HOSPITALIZATION

Hospitalization might be desired for a number of different reasons:

1. If the person is in danger of doing physical harm to himself/herself or to someone else.

2. In cases of chronic alcohol or drug addiction to help the person physically withdraw from using the alcohol/drug.

3. In the case of a psychotic episode where the person is not in touch with reality.

4. To establish or regulate medication.

5. To provide the person with a secure refuge from a particular stressful situation.

6. To give the person the high level of support provided by daily contact with the physician and hospital personnel.

Sometimes hospitalization is necessary before a client/patient can begin work with a therapist. For some people partial hospitalization, either day or night, is adequate. Day hospitalization is also available at some mental health centers.

Even though you have decided that either you or one of your family members needs hospitalization, the final decision will be made by a physician who is

20

on the staff of that hospital following his/her evaluation.

ADDITIONAL LEARNING EXPERIENCES

Other learning experiences that provide opportunities for change and growth are also available in many communities. They may deal with such specific areas as assertiveness training, communications skills, and parent-child relationships as well as a wide range of other subject areas. They are frequently offered through community colleges, universities, religious groups, mental health centers and associations, and other community agencies.

These learning experiences may be ends in themselves, may serve as preludes to therapy, or may be used in conjunction with therapy.

FINAL NOTE

Whatever choice you make, keep in mind that your goal is individual help for you or someone close to you—and that even though you may find the process of finding help like a long and winding road, the goal is well worth your effort.

3

*How Can I Assess
the Credentials
of Social Workers,
Psychologists,
and Psychiatrists?*

We have said that in choosing a therapist you will want to check out and assess his/her credentials. This section is designed to provide information to help you do that.

We are confining the discussion to M.S.W. social workers, Ph.D. psychologists and psychiatrists because of space limitations and because most practicing therapists belong to one of these groups. At the same time we know there are many competent therapists in other fields such as pastoral (and other) counselors, nurse clinicians, social workers of other orientations, M.A. psychologists, and physicians. The ingredients that go into making a good match with a therapist apply in all cases no matter what the discipline of the therapist may be.

Because one therapist is called a social worker, another a psychologist, and a third a psychiatrist, you might reasonably assume that there are some clear-cut differences between them as therapists. In practice there are often more similarities than differences and the dividing lines are becoming more and more blurred.

Differences occur primarily in educational background, training, and regulation, and it is these areas which will be dealt with in this chapter.

As you read, keep in mind that having the education, possessing a license, or being listed in a register or directory is no guarantee that a person will be a good therapist or a good therapist for you.

CLINICAL/PSYCHIATRIC SOCIAL WORKERS— EDUCATION AND CERTIFICATION

When you see the initials ACSW attached to a social worker's name, they stand for membership in the Academy of Certified Social Workers. It means that an individual has attained minimal standards in the general field of social work following a Master's degree. It is entirely optional. It does not relate to any specialty of practice. Social workers are active in many areas. Psychotherapy is only one of them. In order to accurately identify a social worker who has been trained as a therapist, that is, who has been trained in clinical methods and has met minimal criteria accepted by the field for independent practice, a person should determine that a particular social worker is listed in a national registry. There are two such registries serving the field of clinical social work. The *National Registry of Health Care Providers in Clinical Social*

26

Work requires that a professional social worker listed must have met the following criteria:

1. Completed a Master of Social Work or Doctor of Social Work (in some cases Ph.D.) degree with *core of clinical course work* or its demonstrated equivalent and related practice.

2. Completed at least two years or the equivalent of clinical social work experience under the supervision of a clinical social worker.

3. Has agreed to submit to the review of peers on the local clinical peer review and standards committee, or through such mechanisms as may be recognized by the Board of the National Registry.

A second registry is the *NASW Register of Clinical Social Workers.* It has similar requirements except that it does not require a core of clinical course work.

Some states license clinical social workers. One can be fairly assured if a person is licensed in such a state at the time of this writing that they meet the minimum requirements to practice psychotherapy independently.

PSYCHOLOGISTS—EDUCATION AND REGULATION

Psychologists in private practice who offer direct services for a fee are regulated by certification or licensing laws in all fifty states and the District of Columbia. Psychologists who work in laboratories, state or federal institutions, or community agencies may or may not have to be licensed or certified, depending on applicable state law. However, there is a growing trend toward licensing or certifying psychologists who work in these areas.

A certification law generally sets up requirements which must be met by an individual who wants to legally use the title "psychologist." A licensing law also contains specific requirements to be met by those wishing to use the title "psychologist," but usually goes further and sets up a structure to regulate the practice of psychology, such as procedures to be followed for license revocation.

The exact requirements for certification or licensing vary from state to state but generally include meeting certain levels of education, training, and experience and passing a written or oral examination. Most states require a doctoral degree in psychology from an approved university program which meets state standards or standards set by the American Psychological Association (APA). One or two years of supervised experience in an approved setting are usually required. Some states also license or certify psychologists with a Master's degree when they meet certain experience requirements.

Some psychologists achieve diplomate status within

28

the American Board of Professional Psychology (ABPP). "To achieve [this] status requires [completing] at least five years of post-doctoral experience and passing an examination in a special field, such as clinical or counseling" (*Maze*, p. 22).

Participation in a state-approved university program or diplomate status in the ABPP does not guarantee that a psychologist has had clinical or counseling training. So an appropriate question for a psychologist would be: Was your education and experience in a clinical or counseling psychology program? And to an ABPP diplomate: What is your area of specialization? (There are four: clinical, counseling, industrial and organizational, and school.)

The American Psychological Association issues certificates to identify qualified therapists in the United States and lists them in the *National Register of Health Care Service Providers in Psychology*. "Listing requires state licensing [or certification] and agreement by a team of reviewers that the psychologist's work experience involved delivery of direct, preventive, assessment, and therapeutic intervention services to individuals" (APA *Monitor* as quoted in *Maze*, p. 23). While the register does not include all qualified clinical or counseling psychologists, since participation in the project is voluntary and not all qualified therapists elect to be included, it does offer the consumer concise information.

29

PSYCHIATRISTS—EDUCATION,
LICENSING, AND BOARD STATUS

A psychiatrist is a psychotherapist with an M.D. degree from an accredited medical school. As a doctor, he/she must be licensed by the state to practice medicine and, by law, can prescribe medication.

In order to identify a medical doctor who has had additional training in clinical psychiatry, it is necessary to determine if he/she has satisfactorily completed a three-year clinical psychiatric residency in a program approved by the American Medical Association and the American Psychiatric Association. The majority of psychiatrists have completed this kind of residency.

In some state hospitals, and in some smaller communities, there may be doctors who are functioning as psychiatrists on the basis of their own particular interest in the community need and who have had no residency training in psychiatry or an incomplete residency. In larger metropolitan areas, however, most psychiatrists in private practice have completed the three-year clinical psychiatric residency.

Membership in the American Psychiatric Association is an indicator of specialized psychiatric training, since one of its requirements is satisfactory completion of the three-year residency program mentioned above. "[An indicator] of the quality of a residency program is its affiliation with a medical school." *(Maze,* p. 23).

If a psychiatrist is interested in becoming Board Certified, he/she may apply to do so after being in practice for two years following residency. Applicants are required to pass an examination administered by the American Board of Psychiatry and Neurology. "Board certification is usually needed for higher level teaching and hospital jobs" *(Maze,* p. 24).

There are some directories you may find helpful in checking a psychiatrist's credentials. One is the *Biographical Directory of the American Psychiatric Association* which lists its members geographically and notes board certification. Another is the *American Medical Directory,* a three-volume set which lists every M.D. licensed to practice in the United States, and the *Directory of Medical Specialists.* As with all professional directories, the primary problem for the layman is access. It may take considerable perseverance to locate an up-to-date copy of any of the directories mentioned above. Possible sources are your local medical society or public or university libraries.

4

What Can I Expect?

Let's assume that you have now used the information contained in the last two chapters to compile a list of possible therapists or as the source for the name of just one therapist. In either case, you have made a beginning. Now you may be faced with a number of questions. How do I contact the therapist? Will he/she see me? What do I say? What about money? What can I do on the telephone? You may want to try some of these suggested procedures.

The first is to call the therapist's office and tell the secretary something like, "I'm considering going into therapy. Would you please have the therapist call me?" One important point: Use the therapist's secretary only for making appointments or leaving messages. All other dealings should be directly with the therapist.

When the therapist returns your call, he/she will probably be willing to answer some of your questions in a brief telephone conversation—such things as what modes of therapy he/she uses, fees and financial arrangements, length of sessions, and whether or not he/she will be able to see you.

If you and the therapist can get together and an appointment is made, it is entirely appropriate for you to tell him/her you would like to set up three or four appointments "to see if therapy would be helpful for me and if we can work together."

WHAT IS PSYCHOTHERAPY?

So far, we have referred to therapy and the therapeutic process frequently without defining what they are.

A good, all-purpose definition of psychotherapy is hard to come by, but we have put together one that we hope will cover most types of therapy:

Psychotherapy is a process involving a relationship between a person who is seeking to change, grow, and understand himself or herself and his/her interactions with others and a therapist trained to facilitate that process.

Psychotherapy is a talking process, and the client/patient must be willing to talk. If you are not willing to talk to the therapist, not much is going to happen, since even the most skilled therapist does not read minds. Successful therapy requires that you express and share your feelings and thoughts to the best of your ability. There may be things you find embarrassing or painful to discuss—intimate aspects of your life you find difficult to reveal—but it is necessary that you talk openly about them to the therapist.

36

You may experience some discomfort during your first interview with the therapist. Many people do. The discomfort may even continue for the first few sessions. Focusing on areas of emotional pain for therapeutic purposes can cause discomfort. But it is important to distinguish between discomfort caused by what is being talked about (this is quite normal and can even be a sign of growth) and continuing basic discomfort in talking with this particular person, this therapist.

Our intention in introducing the subject of "comfort" here is simply to reassure you that some initial discomfort is not unusual and to make clear to you that even though you may feel uncomfortable, it is important that you not let it prevent you from talking frankly and openly with the therapist.

During the first few interviews, you and the therapist will be jointly evaluating whether therapy is the best course of action. You may want to ask the therapist what he or she sees as your major problem areas (diagnosis)—what the likelihood is of the resolution of those problem areas (prognosis)—and how long he or she expects your therapy to take. These are not always simple or easy questions to answer but, nevertheless, ones you may want to raise. Or perhaps you have already decided for yourself that you *do* need therapy. Either way, it is important that you go into these first sessions on an uncommitted basis. The therapist is going to be evaluating your problems and needs, and whether he/she can work with you. And you will be evaluating whether you can work with this particular therapist.

If after these first few meetings you decide that the match is not a good one, you can tell the therapist so: "This is not working right for me. I really want something different." Discuss with the therapist where you might go, because at this point he/she may have some good ideas about another therapist with whom you will match better. Keep on looking for a good match until you find one.

PSYCHOLOGICAL TESTING

Some therapists use psychological testing as a diagnostic tool to get underneath the immediate pressing complaint and to better understand how this symptom fits into the overall context of the client/patient's personality pattern.

You will want to ask which psychological tests will be used, what the purpose of each of these tests is and how it relates to you, and the cost of each test. The cost of testing varies, so if cost is an important consideration to you, tell the therapist. With this information, you can determine whether or not you want to have the testing done. If you decide to go ahead with the tests, you have the right to have the results interpreted to you. (See Chapter 7 for additional information about psychological tests.)

Should you want to postpone testing with a particular therapist until you are sure you are going to work with him/her, it is entirely appropriate to tell the therapist that this is what you have decided. If you should change therapists after testing, it is also appropriate to ask to have your tests forwarded to your new therapist.

STAGES OF THE THERAPEUTIC PROCESS

All therapy, whether short-term or long-term, proceeds through several stages. In the initial stages of both short-term and long-term therapy the client/patient and the therapist are looking each other over, testing each other out, and there may be some discomfort for the client/patient. The therapy process moves into a second stage when the client/patient really decides to trust the therapist, willingly puts himself/herself in a vulnerable position, and lets the therapist become important. In long-term therapy the client/patient may also feel a degree of dependency at this stage and idealize the therapist, becoming upset if he/she or other people find flaws in the therapist.

In both short-term and long-term therapy, as the client/patient achieves his/her goals and is ready to terminate, the therapist begins to recede into the background and other people and other activities become more important than therapy. In long-term therapy there may also be a period of aggravation or hostility as a part of the letting-go or there may just be a feeling of sadness in giving up a relationship that has been an important part of your life.

INDIVIDUAL AND GROUP THERAPY

Most of what we have discussed above implies that you and your therapist will meet regularly for individual therapy interviews. This may be true, especially during the first few sessions, but many therapists also employ group psychotherapy where several clients/patients meet with the therapist at the same time. Group therapy, like individual therapy, varies with the orientation of the therapist. If you are considering group therapy, you may want to ask the therapist about the size of the group, whether there will be a co-therapist, how long the sessions will be, and what the customary fee is.

Working in a group situation can often provide specific advantages for the client/patient. A realization that others are in much the "same boat" may reduce anxiety and make it easier to express deeper feelings. Listening to others and exchanging ideas with them can stimulate you to recall and relive your own experiences. Other members may suggest new ways of approaching and solving problems. By ex-

40

pressing yourself safely in a group situation you may dissipate some of the feelings of hostility or guilt that may be standing in your way. Acceptance by the group can provide an opportunity to test and reinforce new ways of behaving and new relationships.

Whether you will benefit most from individual or group therapy or a combination of the two is a decision that should be made jointly by you and your therapist.

COLLABORATIVE RELATIONSHIPS

You may want to determine if a prospective therapist has a collaborative relationship with a physician and/or another mental health professional.

A collaborative relationship is one in which a therapist has an arrangement with a physician and/or another mental health professional within his/her own field or another discipline for specific purposes. For example, a social worker or a psychologist might decide that a client would benefit from medication and have a collaborative relationship with a physician for this purpose. A psychiatrist might have such a relationship with a psychologist for the purpose of administering psychological tests. Another obvious use of the collaborative relationship is when one therapist takes over for another during vacations, in case of illness, or at other times when the primary therapist is not available. Some other reasons for hav-

41

ing collaborative relationships include: consultation (probably the most frequent reason), hospitalization, insurance purposes, to take a social history, or referral for therapy.

OTHER FORMS OF THERAPY

This book deals primarily with psychotherapy. Sometimes other forms of therapy are used instead of, in addition to, or in preparation for, psychotherapy, such as chemotherapy (medication), electroshock therapy, and milieu therapy (hospitalization). Hospitalization was discussed in Chapter 2 and electroshock therapy and chemotherapy will be discussed in Chapter 6.

5

How Can I Make Therapy an Investment with Positive Returns?

MAKING A GOOD MATCH

It has become clear by now that the relationship between you and your therapist is important if the therapeutic process is to be effective. So the time and effort you spend in working to achieve a good "match" is well worth the investment.

Consider any potential therapist as a human being possessing a combination of personal qualities and therapeutic skills. The kinds of qualities and the level of skills vary from one therapist to another and some qualities may be more important to you than others, but there are certain qualities we feel are common to most good therapists.

The first and most important quality a therapist should have is a sense of caring and a feeling of genuine concern for those with whom he/she works —the ability to show "unconditional positive regard." The therapist who has this quality is felt to be non-judgmental and noncritical so that you are better able to really trust him/her and go on to the self-disclosure necessary for effective therapy.

Second, the therapist must be willing to make a commitment to you, the client/patient. People entering therapy may be uncommitted to themselves and have to rely for a time on the commitment the therapist is willing to make to them until they are in a position to accept this responsibility for themselves.

Third, the therapist should be clear, straightforward, and sincere, so you feel that what the therapist says corresponds to what he/she really thinks or feels.

Fourth, the therapist should be dependable, especially in regard to scheduled appointments and agreements.

Fifth, the therapist should be ethical and should treat your revelations of self and others as confidential. A clear understanding of what the therapist means by confidentiality is essential since the specific limits of it may vary from situation to situation. For example, under some circumstances colleagues may informally consult with one another, and in some agencies internal staff discussion of client/patient problems and progress is a regular procedure. In general you can expect confidentiality, but different therapists may define it in different ways, so if confidentiality is a particular concern for you, discuss it fully and frankly with the therapist.

All of the qualities discussed above are found to a greater or lesser degree in any competent therapist, but the weight you attach to a particular quality or qualities will be a strong factor in deciding whether or not a specific therapist is a good match for you.

Another important part of the relationship between you and the therapist is *how* he/she relates to you. Is his/her style of relating acceptable to you? Does he/she have something that really stands in the way of your being able to reveal yourself? What kind of personality do you respond to? Supportive? Confronting? Enthusiastic? Gentle? Do you feel comfortable with the therapist? Is your personal chemistry compatible? Are there "good vibes" between you?

Some clients/patients have told us the following qualities were individually important to them: communicating a high degree of sensitivity and intuition; being able to serve effectively as a mirror in which you can more clearly see and understand yourself; possessing a good sense of humor. How well the therapist's style relates to you and your needs is a question you alone can answer, something you'll have to feel yourself. All we have done here is suggest some areas to consider in making that assessment.

Consideration of a therapist's skills as a mental health professional can begin with his/her credentials. Therapists should be adequately trained in the discipline from which they come, should be able to effectively employ that training and have the capacity and willingness to impart information. You may want to ask the therapist simple, informational questions about education, clinical experience, licensing or certification, length of time in practice, etc. But you'll want to ask yourself questions as well, including one that will help you judge the therapist's level of skill: does what he/she says and does make sense to me? You'll want to decide how well the therapist "does what he/she does," how it can help you, and whether or not you can respond to it.

Your particular needs will play a large part in arriving at a good match with a therapist. They will be important in considering the mode of therapy a particular therapist employs and how well it fits your needs. A brief description of several therapy modes can be found in Chapter 6.

Business arrangements may be an important consideration depending on your financial situation. Some questions you may want to ask the therapist are: What is your fee? When must the fee be paid? Will you negotiate a reduced fee if I have limited financial resources? Do you accept Medicare, Medicaid, or insurance payments? How long a session will I have? Do you have sessions of varying lengths and fees? How will I be charged if I miss an appointment? Do you charge for telephone calls? You may also want to ask: May I call you at times other than your normal working hours? How often and under what circumstances may I call? Is there someone I may call in an emergency if you are not available? Will you be seeing/contacting my spouse and/or family?

You may have personal preferences such as age, sex, or length of time a prospective therapist has been practicing. You may want to know the therapist's attitudes about certain issues that are very important to you: religion, women's issues, cultural values, lifestyles, divorce, abortion, sex, drugs, or any others. Check them out with the therapist early so you can determine whether or not they would interfere with the flow of therapy. To clarify the therapist's attitudes, you have the right to ask any questions, even very personal ones. However, the therapist also has the right not to answer. If a therapist should decline to answer any of your questions, it does not necessarily mean that the answer is negative. But if openness in the therapeutic relationship is important to you, you may want to assess a refusal to answer in terms of your needs. It may be important to you to look at the reasons for your questions as well.

There is no foolproof method we can give you to use in making a good match—no guarantees, no "check lists." What we have provided here is background material that can be useful in framing questions both for yourself and a prospective therapist— and the assurance that you have the right to ask them. It is *your* right. It is *your* match. It is *your* therapy.

MAKING A CLEAR CONTRACT

There have always been implicit or unspoken agreements between therapists and clients/

patients—an understanding of their roles in the therapy process and the relationships between them. It may have been as simple as "I will come to see you and pay you money and you will work with me."

Today, changes are taking place in the mental health field, and explicit, or clearly thought-out, mutually articulated contracts between therapists and clients/patients are coming into more general use as a part of the therapeutic process. A contract as we use the term here is not a legally binding document but rather an agreement about what the goals of therapy are, what the therapist is going to do, and what the client/patient is going to do. It could include:

1. Establishing what the client/patient wants out of therapy.

2. Response from the therapist in terms of whether or not he/she can be helpful in achieving those goals.

3. An outline of what the treatment procedure is going to be, particularly in terms of time and money.

Use of a clear contract can "establish a mutual and routine accountability between [client] patient and therapist," as well as providing a method for measuring the outcome of therapy. "The contract makes clear to both parties that the therapy process is a mutual effort which entails mutual responsibilities. . . . Goals will differ from person to person, as will the methods thought worthwhile exploring. The essence of the contract is that those responsibilities, those methods, those goals be spelled out in advance with a clear understanding by both parties" (*Maze*, pp. 35–36).

As preparation for making the contract you may want to organize in your mind what you consider to be your specific problems and possibly even set them down on paper along with any questions you may have for the therapist. Making a brief outline increases the chance that you will more easily get down to specifics.

Your contract can also address itself to the business arrangements between you and the therapist. "Sometimes misunderstandings occur about [such things as] finances, third-party payment[s] . . . or hours simply because of failure to discuss them in advance" (*Maze*, p. 38).

"The length of time for making the contract—the negotiation—may vary, but one to three sessions should probably be enough" (*Maze*, p. 37). As you set your goals, they may become clearer to you and the therapist may not be what you originally thought were the key issues. When goals are not clear the therapist can often help you develop them more clearly.

One point is very important: In no way are you or the therapist locked into a particular contract. It can be renegotiated at any time. In ongoing therapy the contract is always subject to review. It should change as goals are reached or are redefined, or as other parts of the contract change and need revision.

Some therapists are familiar with the concept of a therapeutic contract and will be willing to enter into this kind of agreement either verbally or in writing. Others prefer only a verbal agreement. Still others do not use explicit contracts at all. In considering a prospective therapist you will want to assess whether or not he/she will enter into a contract in terms of its value to you. An explicit contract is not an absolute prerequisite for effective therapy, but it has been found to be an extremely useful therapeutic tool for many people, both therapists and clients/patients.

WAYS TO FACILITATE THERAPY

Anything you can do to facilitate therapy will make it more productive for you. Two of the most obvious ways are to keep your scheduled appointments and arrive on time. Once there, talk. Talk about things it may be difficult for you to discuss, both positive and negative. One of the areas where you may experience difficulty is in talking to your therapist about feelings you may have about him/her—hurt, anger, sexual, disappointment, tenderness, admiration, envy, love, protectiveness, or whatever they might be. Experiencing feelings like these is very common and should be dealt with openly; otherwise they will interfere with the therapy process. Keep in mind that while you are in therapy, the primary place for discharging feelings and for self-disclosing should be during the therapeutic session. If you do it with friends and relatives instead, the session may be less painful but it may also be less effective. If someone you love is in therapy, encourage him/her to talk to the therapist about the things that he or she finds troubling.

Some other ways you can help facilitate therapy are by being willing: to be honest, to make a real commitment to the therapy process, to think, to discuss, to receive and give feedback (positive and negative), to confront and be confronted, to risk, to take responsibilities, to ask for and accept help, to listen and evaluate what is said, to try new methods and new patterns of behavior, to give up inappropriate ways of relating, to recognize your strengths as well as your weaknesses, to disagree when necessary, to ask for clarification if you don't understand, and to keep your contract.

Another way to facilitate therapy is to check out from time to time what progress has been made, what goals have been achieved, and what direction therapy should now take.

One of the best ways to make therapy more productive is to examine yourself for openness in the therapeutic relationship. The sooner games, defenses, and façades can be discarded, the sooner effective movement will occur.

53

6

What Do I Need to Know about Different Modes of Therapy?

This chapter consists of brief descriptions of some modes of psychotherapy. They are intended to convey some of the main points of the modes described and to give some indication of the diversity of the modes of therapy used by psychotherapists. Many therapists use a combination of two or more modes in their practices. You may want to get more information about the specific mode(s) of therapy that a prospective therapist uses, especially if this is one of your prime considerations in choosing a particular therapist.

ADLERIAN

Adlerians believe that individuals often engage in a wide variety of unrealistic self-defeating behaviors (relentless search for power, prestige, fame, wealth) in order to compensate or overcome deep feelings of inadequacy and inferiority. Through the therapeutic relationship the therapist plays an active role in assisting the client/patient to substitute realistic for unrealistic goals and in achieving more personally rewarding relationships in the home and community. The person comes to learn about his/her basic lifestyle in order to reshape his/her life.

BEHAVIOR MODIFICATION (THERAPY)

Behavior modification therapy is any one of a number of specific treatment methods designed to directly change behavior itself rather than focus on the cause of the behavior. Behavior therapists believe that it is not necessary for the client/patient to know the causes or reasons for his/her behavior in order for change to occur. The first step in this form of therapy is to identify the specific (target) behavior to work on, such as a particular fear or self-defeating behavior. A system of rewards (i.e., control of reinforcement) may be established to increase the probability that desired behavior will occur. The therapist may assist the client/patient in overcoming a fear by helping the person gradually get accustomed to small representations of the feared object or situation (i.e., systematic desensitization). In order to overcome passive behavior a client/patient might receive assertiveness training. The therapy can be applied in treating certain phobias and sexual dysfunctions.

BIO-FEEDBACK

Bio-feedback is a type of treatment that utilizes scientifically designed equipment to monitor and report to the client/patient certain body phenomena such as blood pressure or body temperature. The premise is that the individual can learn to control physical processes or responses and reduce symptoms such as tension or migraine headache, high blood pressure and hypertension.

BODY THERAPIES

The use of the body as well as the mind in releasing harmful emotions and expanding mental awareness is becoming increasingly popular. *Rolfing, the Alexander Technique, Feldenkrais Method* and *Reichian* (or Neo-Reichian) are four such body therapies. *Rolfing,* formulated by Ida Rolf, employs deep muscle manipulation in order to release damaging emotional memories. Moshe Feldenkrais, founder of the *Feldenkrais Method,* has developed over 30,000 body exercises, the purpose of which is expanded mental awareness and increased physical dexterity. The *Alexander Technique,* founded by Matthias Alexander, stresses a balanced physical use of the body resulting in the least amount of tension and stress. *Reichian* (or *Neo-Reichian*) is a form of therapy based on the early writings and work of Wilhelm Reich. A premise in the present-day form of Reichian Therapy is that problems in living are due to the blocking of expression of feelings. These blocks to feeling are physically localized within the body. The individual must release

59

the blocks to feeling and allow the feelings to be expressed and experienced. Through structured exercises the individual experiences deep emotional release and learns to deal with feelings appropriately.

CLIENT-CENTERED THERAPY

Client-Centered Therapy is a method of treatment developed by Carl Rogers and his associates in the early 1950s. Its purpose is to have the client/patient, rather than the therapist, arrive at insights and make interpretations. The focus is with the individual's present attitudes and behavior rather than with early childhood experiences and history. The therapist creates an atmosphere in which the person feels his or her own significance. The client/patient assumes responsibility for individual change and growth.

ECLECTIC

Therapy which utilizes theory and technique from more than one of the generally accepted therapeutic modes is called eclectic. A therapist combines techniques he/she believes to be appropriate or suitable for an individual client/patient. The approach is flexible, but with purpose and intent.

ELECTROSHOCK THERAPY

Electroshock therapy is a medical form of treatment primarily useful with some severely depressed patients who have failed to respond to other forms of treatment.

The patient is first sedated with a muscle-relaxant sedative. A measured amount of electrical current is applied to certain areas of the brain through electrodes which are placed on the temples. The shock is designed to produce a convulsion which is followed by a brief period of unconsciousness. Similar to an operation, electroshock therapy leaves no memory of the treatment. No one understands *how* the shock produces a therapeutic effect although many explanations have been offered.

While shock therapy is sometimes good at interrupting a depressive process when nothing else will, it does not give patients any better skills or tools for dealing with people or situations in their lives. If a person needs to make these kinds of changes, another type of therapy is needed instead of or in addition to shock therapy. Also there are risks and limitations to shock therapy, and memory disturbance is one of these. We recommend a thorough discussion of the risks and limitations with the psychiatrist.

If a series of shock treatments is advised, but either the patient or the family would prefer another form of treatment, it would be quite appropriate to ask for a consultation with another psychiatrist for a second opinion.

ENCOUNTER GROUPS

Encounter groups are a form of intensive small group experience in which participants are encouraged to interact mainly on an emotional level. Emphasis is upon personal growth through expanding awareness, exploration of self and relationships with others, and release of self-defeating inhibitions. Encounter groups meet on a weekly basis or in a lengthy marathon session which lasts over a single weekend. They are best used for enrichment rather than treatment. Not all encounter groups are led by trained psychotherapists.

EXISTENTIAL THERAPY

Existential Therapy focuses on helping the person find personal meaning and significance in life through exploring in depth the personal relationship between self and others. Emphasis is placed upon making the person more aware of the potential for growth and change through discovering how choices can limit and/or expand human possibilities. The analysis of the relationship between the person and the therapist is of special significance in the treatment process.

FAMILY THERAPY

Family Therapy is a form of therapy in which the entire family is treated as a therapeutic unit. The idea is that family members each influence one another and consequently contribute to the problems of one or more members. Family therapy is uniquely appropriate with cases of marital discord and problems with children. One or more psychotherapists may be involved. Therapy is directed toward helping family members express and clarify their feelings about one another and work out more effective ways of relating to one another.

FREUDIAN
(SEE PSYCHOANALYSIS)

FEMINIST

This is therapy in which the therapist is contemporary in his/her awareness of the feminist movement today. The therapist's feminine-consciousness is of a high level and the therapist is aware of the subtle (and more obvious) forms of discrimination women receive currently. Although the type of therapy utilized may be of any school of thought, the interaction between therapist and client/patient is nonsexist (unbiased, unstereotyped) in its direction and solution of problems.

GESTALT

Gestalt is a type of therapy developed by Fritz Perls which focuses on the individual becoming aware of his/her whole personality. "Unfinished business" (unresolved conflict) is worked through and the individual becomes aware of feelings that were formerly blocked. Techniques used include: acting out fantasies or dreams, and giving a voice to the two sides of one's conflict. The therapy emphasizes quality contact with others and the environment. The past is dealt with only as it emerges in the "here and now."

HUMANISTIC

Humanistic psychotherapy is a term which encompasses a wide range of therapies and techniques, all of which emphasize certain beliefs. Humanists believe that each individual strives for "self-actualization" (i.e., self-knowledge and the realization of one's full potential in relationship to self and others). Several techniques are utilized in achieving self-actualization including: Gestalt therapy, encounter groups and sensory awareness training.

HYPNO THERAPY

Hypno Therapy is a process by which a therapist induces a state of altered attention in a client/patient

64

by using body relaxation and/or concentration on a thought or visual image. The purpose of hypnosis is often to increase the client/patient's susceptibility to suggestion in order to bring about behavioral changes (e.g., to stop smoking or overeating, or reduce fears for phobic reactions). Not all hypnotists are trained psychotherapists.

JUNG (JUNGIAN)

Jungian therapy is based on the writings and theories of Carl Jung (1875–1961). Jung's analytical psychology was in many ways like Freudian therapy although Jung placed less emphasis on sexual drives in emotional disorders. Jung's writings are mystical in nature and are filled with unique terminology and concepts. These concepts are utilized in therapy to clarify and explain processes going on within the individual in daily living experiences. The aim of the treatment process is a better integration of the personality through a joint effort of the client/patient and therapist in a situation which encourages spontaneous and open confrontations and analysis of dreams.

PHARMACOTHERAPY (CHEMOTHERAPY)

Pharmacotherapy involves the use of specially prescribed drugs in the treatment of emotional problems. Essentially, these drugs fall into two major categories:

65

1. Tranquilizers to relieve tension, anxiety, nervousness, agitation.

2. Antidepressants (mood elevators or energizers) to relieve depression.

These drugs are used primarily to alleviate or modify distressing and painful feelings. The person is made to feel more comfortable, enabling him/her to meet everyday responsibilities in a more effective manner. Frequently psychoactive drugs are used in conjunction with other forms of therapy. For a more complete discussion of Chemotherapy, see Chapter 8.

PSYCHOANALYSIS (FREUDIAN)

Psychoanalysis is a mode of treatment based on the concepts of Sigmund Freud (1856–1939). A fundamental premise in Freudian therapy is that conflict areas outside the conscious awareness of the individual have been repressed and must be brought into awareness. Free association is a technique used by clients/patients in analysis to get in touch with unconscious thoughts and feelings. Dream interpretation is also used to uncover and identify formerly unconscious material. The analysis of the client/patient–therapist relationship is of crucial significance in the treatment. Psychoanalysis is a long-term form of therapy (often several years) involving three or more sessions weekly.

PSYCHOANALYTIC PSYCHOTHERAPY

Psychoanalytic psychotherapy is a simplified and shorter method of treatment than psychoanalysis based on modified principles of psychoanalysis. The goals are symptom resolution and personality change. The techniques include interpretations and confrontations. This method can deal with a wide range of problems. The focus of therapy is the client/patient's life situation and secondarily the client/patient–therapist relationship. Psychoanalytic psychotherapy may be used for short-term treatments.

PSYCHOSURGERY

Since the movie *One Flew Over the Cuckoo's Nest,* many people have developed fears about psychosurgery or lobotomy. Psychosurgery is an extremely controversial form of treatment using standard neurosurgical procedures to sever certain pathways in the brain in the hope of interrupting thought and behavior patterns that are highly incapacitating to the individual. Because the results are not wholly predictable, responsible advocates of psychosurgery consider it only after many other conventional methods of treatment have proved unsuccessful. It is not a standard mode of therapy.

67

RATIONAL-EMOTIVE THERAPY (RET)

Rational-Emotive Therapy is a form of therapy developed by Albert Ellis. This approach assumes that a great deal of emotional suffering is due to unrealistic goals and irrational thoughts. Essentially it is believed that we interpret everyday events and that our interpretations lead to certain feelings. WHAT YOU THINK DETERMINES WHAT YOU FEEL. In order to change feelings one must change the negative (irrational) thoughts that initiate and maintain the feelings. These thoughts include sentences such as "one should be competent in all respects all the time." The therapist challenges these ideas and encourages the client/patient to take a more "rational" view of himself/herself. Rational-Behavior Training (RBT), a further development of RET, focuses on an explicit program which includes training in rational thinking and behavior change.

REALITY THERAPY

Reality Therapy, "a pragmatic 'here and now' approach [developed by William Glasser] emphasizes how to cope with daily environment, happenings, [and] relationships rather than childhood or infantile experiences. Reality therapy is coaching on how to deal with a hostile environment" (*Maze*, p. 65). The therapist helps the client/patient understand the consequences of possible courses of action in order to decide on a realistic solution or goal.

SULLIVANIAN

Sullivanians view the therapeutic process as an interpersonal relationship in which the therapist, as a participating observer, helps the client/patient see how he distorts and misinterprets events. The belief is that once long-standing distortions are resolved the person will live a more satisfying and productive life.

TRANSACTIONAL ANALYSIS

Transactional Analysis is a theory of personality and form of therapy developed by Eric Berne. It uses four major methods to understand human behavior: (1) Structural Analysis, which defines and describes three ego states present and interacting within each individual, P (Parent—values), A (Adult—reason), C (Child—feelings); (2) Transactional Analysis, which describes and explains interactions in terms of the ego states involved; (3) Racket and Game Analysis, which clarifies and explains repetitive kinds of transactions which result in bad feeling payoffs; (4) Script Analysis, which identifies the life plan an individual may be following.

Several new methods have evolved; among them are corrective parenting and reparenting. These interventions are used to decrease the influence of harmful or ineffective parental messages and to substitute adaptive and positive parental influence. Another new method is "redecision therapy." It is based on the theory that children make decisions about the course of their lives prematurely. The early scene is relived and a new, more appropriate redecision is made.

7

What Do I Need to Know about Psychological Tests?

Although there are hundreds of psychological tests, most fall into the following three categories: (1) *intelligence tests* which determine an individual score known as an intelligence quotient (IQ); (2) *personality tests* which help identify an individual's personality characteristics; and (3) *tests which determine if organic or physical factors may be affecting personality or performance.* Some of the more frequently used tests in each category include: (1) for intelligence—the Stanford Binet Intelligence Test, the Wechsler Adult Intelligence Scale (WAIS), the Wechsler Intelligence Scale for Children (WISC); (2) for personality—the Minnesota Multiphasic Personality Inventory (MMPI), the Rorschach (ink-blot) Test, the Thematic Apperception Test (TAT), and various Sentence Completion tests; (3) for organicity—the Bender Gestalt Test.

The time required to take a particular psychological test varies from a few minutes up to two to three hours. Some tests are of the paper-and-pencil kind and may be taken by the client/patient alone or administered by someone other than a psychologist.

Other tests are administered only by a psychologist. Usually, more than one test is given. A complete diagnostic work-up may include the use of several tests.

See Chapter 4 for other factors to consider regarding psychological testing.

8

What Do I Need to Know about Medication?

There are several medications used because of their effects on emotions, feelings, or behavior. Should your therapist decide that medication (chemotherapy) would be helpful to you, don't think of yourself as being "sicker" than someone who does not take medication. Chemotherapy is a legitimate treatment in itself and is frequently used in conjunction with other forms of therapy. In order for your medication to be most effective, it is important that you take it as prescribed. Don't adjust dosage or stop taking your medication because you are feeling better.

Anytime medication is prescribed, you should inform your doctors and dentist of any known allergies or illnesses you may have and especially of any medications you may already be taking. Carry your medications to show or have a list. Your doctor will be particularly interested in knowing of glaucoma, prostatic problems, high blood pressure, and drinking problems—present or past. These commonly have significant interactions with psychiatric medications. Since individuals react differently in terms of their tolerance of medication, ask your doctor what sort of side effects you might experience. If your reaction differs markedly, let him/her know right away.

Never, never mix medications without your doctor's permission. Combining alcohol, prescription drugs, and/or across-the-counter medications can be dangerous, even deadly. If you are aware that someone you love is mixing or overusing medications and/or alcohol, call his or her physician or therapist.

If you feel that, in your therapy, too much emphasis is being placed on medication and your other needs are not being met, discuss these concerns with your therapist. Or if you are receiving no medication and believe you might benefit from it, tell your therapist. In either case, if you are still not satisfied, seek a consultation with another therapist for a second opinion.

The following list of medications is by no means complete, but contains the most commonly used drugs.

GROUP I: MAJOR TRANQUILIZERS OR
ANTI-PSYCHOTIC AGENTS

These may best be described as "helping to keep your thinking just a little bit straighter." This group has been of great benefit in major emotional illness. While sometimes sedative in their effect, these medications do not exert their primary effect through sedation and are not considered addictive, nor does tolerance develop for the desired therapeutic effect. They are used in widely varying doses. (Much higher doses are often used when illness is severe enough to require hospitalization.)

Side effects include sedation, involuntary muscle movements, stiffness, restlessness, dry mouth, stuffy nose, skin rash, hypersensitivity to the sun, and weight gain.

A. Phenothiazines: Thorazine, Stelazine, Mellaril, Prolixin, Navane.

B. Butrophenone: Haldol.

GROUP II: ANTIDEPRESSANTS

May best be described as "giving back control of your mood instead of the mood controlling you."

A. Tricyclics: Elavil, Tofranil, Norpramin, Pertofrane, Sinequan.

These medications do a reasonably good job of interrupting depressive episodes, and are usually the first medication used. The effects are not necessarily immediate and seem to increase at two or three weeks. An increase in dosage may be needed to take full advantage of the medication. Side effects, however, do start with the first dose. Some are: fainting and dizziness, blurred vision, dry mouth, urinary retention, and tremors. While abuse and addiction have not been a problem, they should not be stopped suddenly, as there is a rebound effect.

B. MAO inhibitors: Parnate, Marplan, Nardil.

This group is reasonably effective and would be more widely used were it not for their part in causing high blood pressure attacks. This is known to occur in relationship with certain foods, and dietary restrictions need to be well understood.

GROUP III: ANTI-ANXIETY AGENTS, SEDATIVES, MINOR TRANQUILIZERS, SLEEPING PILLS

These medications exert their main effect by making people less anxious, less caring, or sleepy. In large enough doses, they will all put people to sleep. These medications are widely used by all of the medical specialties, frequently in combination with other medication, such as for ulcers. These are a great benefit to mankind in distress; however, this group is subject to developing tolerance with potential dependence, withdrawal effects, abuse, and addiction. This is a function of dosage, time, and the individual; most people will not allow themselves to be addicted. These medications are basically only for short-term use; in time they lose their effectiveness and may become the cause of the very symptoms they were used

80

to relieve. A sign of trouble is a need to keep increasing the dosage to relieve symptoms.

Caution is advisable in driving, operating machinery, or working in high places. Combinations with other drugs, and especially alcohol, may produce unexpected or dangerous sedation (sleepiness). In excess, they produce symptoms of intoxication, unsteady gait, slurred speech, memory trouble, and sleepiness. All of this group can produce or aggravate depression.

A. Valium, Librium, Tranxene, Librax.

The most prescribed medications in the country, they are used to relieve anxiety. They produce less sedation than some and are relatively safe.

B. Barbiturates: phenobarbital, Luminal, Donnatal, Mebaral, Pamine.

In low doses, these are used for daytime sedation. They are frequently combined with medication for other purposes, especially stomach and colon disorders.

Meprobamate: Miltown, Equinil, Equagesic.

Nonbarbiturates that have a very similar effect.

C. Sleeping Medications

1. Barbiturates in higher doses: Amytal, Nembutal, Seconal.

These have been in use for fifty years; usefulness is limited by developing tolerance in two to four weeks.

2. Nonbarbiturates: Chloral Hydrate, Placidyl,

Noludar, Quaalude, Sopor, Parest.

3. Dalmane: May be one of the safer sleeping medications.

D. Alcohol

Although not a prescription item, it shares the general properties of the group. It is the most used and abused sedative in the country, and is included for completeness.

GROUP IV: LITHIUM CARBONATE

Lithium is in a class by itself. It has proved remarkably useful in treatment and prevention of repeated mood swings. While we are still in the process of defining the uses of lithium, it was first used in treating manic episodes in manic-depressive illness. Repeated blood level determinations are used to control dosage. Side effects include tremor, upset stomach, and diarrhea. If blood levels get too high, slurring speech, staggering, and sleepiness occur.

GROUP V: STIMULANTS: BENZEDRINE, DEXEDRINE, DESOXYN, RITALIN HYDROCHLORIDE TABLETS

Used in treating narcolepsy and hyperactive children, they have occasionally had some brief value in managing depression. They have long been used in treating obesity with a rather notable lack of success.

82

Because of extensive abuse, their use has been increasingly restricted by the Food and Drug Administration. They appear in the mental health scene more as a problem in abuse than a therapeutic agent.

GROUP VI: ANTI-PARKINSON DRUGS: ARTANE, COGENTIN, BENADRYL, AKINETON, TREMIN TABLETS, KEMADRIN.

Thorazine and medications in Group I frequently offer enough needed help (such as being able to stay out of the hospital) as to make their use desirable in spite of their side effects. In such situations, these anti-side-effect medications can be used to relieve or reduce the involuntary muscle movements, stiffness, and agitation.

GROUP VII: MISCELLANEOUS

A. Inderal—a cardiac medication which stops the tremor secondary to lithium. It may prove useful in other ways also.

B. Antabuse—useful to alcoholics who *want* help in avoiding drinking. It is not to be used without the patient's knowledge and instruction. If combined with any form of alcohol, it can produce a dangerous reaction.

C. Methadone—Useful in managing heroin narcotic addiction, usually only through special clinics. It is a narcotic and addictive; however, its use has allowed many people to lead a much more normal life than was possible any other way.

9

What Do I Need to Know about Medical Insurance?

Most medical insurance policies provide at least some coverage for mental health services. Generally there are three ways that a particular policy may provide coverage: (1) for hospital-related expenses; (2) for professional fees which are covered on a separate schedule; (3) through major medical (extra insurance designed to cover catastrophic illness). A policy may provide coverage in one, two, or all three ways. Policies also frequently make a difference between inpatient care and outpatient services. At times it's very difficult to know just how much and in what ways a policy will provide coverage.

To find out just what kind of coverage a particular policy may provide, it's a good idea to read the policy or a summary outlining the benefits. After this material has been read (it frequently raises more questions than one had to begin with) you may need to get more information and clarification. If it's a group policy, contact the personnel office or the individual in charge of administering the policy. If it is an individual policy, contact the agent who sold it. A third option would be to contact the customer service department of the insurance company itself. The number of the policy and group is important to know because many companies, particularly Blue Cross–Blue Shield, have many different policies, each with different limits of coverage.

It's a good idea to tell the therapist (or office person handling insurance claims) if insurance is to be used. It may be that they can help determine the benefits available. It is also important for the client/patient to know whether the therapist will take an assignment of insurance benefits in lieu of direct payment or whether the therapist expects to be paid immediately with the client/patient collecting from the insurance company. All hospitals take assignment of benefits, although some may require a cash deposit if benefits are unknown or particularly weak. In any event, usually the therapist and/or hospital must fill out and sign insurance claim forms. Occasionally insurance companies will simply accept documentation of the service and charges in order to reimburse the client/patient if fees have already been paid. A lot of people are surprised when they use their insurance because they did not understand how little or how much coverage they had, how little or how much the company would pay, and who or when the insurance company would pay. While inpatient benefits are usually fairly extensive and quite common in medical policies, outpatient benefits vary greatly. It is important to determine the rate of payment, the number of sessions or length of time, what kind of therapist can be paid, whether or not the services of a nonmedical therapist need to have prior recommendation by a physician, whether or not a diagnosis needs to be made by a physician, etc. If mental health services are covered, one can usually take for granted that psychiatrists' fees are covered. The degree to which the services of a clinical psychologist or clinical/psychiatric social worker are covered may vary. In some cases other types of services may also be covered.

Since a client/patient needs to determine in advance whether the services of a particular therapist can be paid by an insurance policy, it may be useful to know that certain psychologists and clinical/psychiatric social workers are being recognized by insurance companies. In order to assist in recognizing these individuals and to document their credentials, national registries have been developed. These registries are available to insurance companies and are also usually in the hands of any therapist listed therein. In questionable situations, an individual listed in a health care registry stands a better chance of having fees covered than one who is not listed. Aside from insurance coverage, the fact that an individual is listed in such a registry will help determine the clinical qualifications and credentials of the therapist.

Mental health therapists sometimes provide services that are not considered "health" services and may not be covered in an insurance policy. In a very few instances marriage counseling is covered, but usually it is not. Frequently interviews with people who are not identified as the client/patient are not covered.

Medicare (Social Security recipients) and Medicaid (state medical card) can be handled just like regular insurance; however, not all eligible therapists will accept Medicare/Medicaid payments and this should be clarified before therapy is begun. For those who have a tie-in plan there may be supplemental benefits. With Medicaid, the number from the card is taken by the hospital, physician, or mental health center and claims are made with the state paying the provider of services at a fixed rate. The fixed rate must be accepted as full payment. The provider of services cannot bill the client/patient for the difference between the fixed rate and the provider's customary rate or fee.

In short, check out insurance thoroughly in advance to be sure that maximum benefits are obtained without unpleasant surprises.

10

What Do I Do if I Feel Stuck?

Successful therapy requires a substantial amount of work by the client/patient. Some of that work involves spotting obstacles which get in the way of the flow of therapy and knowing what to do about the obstacles when you become aware of them.

INEPT THERAPIST

One such obstacle would be an inept therapist, so being able to recognize ineptness is important. Here are some suggestions about what to look for:

1. A person who is rigid and limited, who tends to stereotype people and their problems across the board. This kind of therapist generally is unable to deal with each person as an individual, but instead has a programmed style that is used for everyone. If the program fits your needs, then there is no problem. If if it does not fit your needs, you will want to seek another therapist.

2. A therapist who consistently exercises poor judgment—for example, putting an emotionally fragile person into an inappropriately confronting situation.

3. A therapist who is untrustworthy: doesn't keep appointments, agreements, contracts, etc.

4. A therapist who relates to the client/patient in a deprecating way, consistently devaluing or discounting the person.

5. A therapist who repeatedly lets personal issues stand in the way of relating to the client/patient. Therapists are human beings and do have unresolved issues in their own lives which may at times get in the way. Give your therapist room for that occasionally, but if you consistently feel that the session is more therapeutic for the therapist than for you, that the therapist's personal problems, issues, or concerns are being dealt with more than your own, it indicates ineptness.

This list isn't intended to be exhaustive but to offer some guidelines to help you protect yourself against incompetence. If you conclude your therapist is inept, it is up to you to terminate the relationship and seek out a good match with a competent therapist.

RESISTANCE

Another obstacle—one of the most commonly experienced in the therapeutic process—is "resistance." Here we use the word in a technical sense, so let's look at what meaning it carries in the therapy situation.

Many people experience pain when working on

certain issues in their lives. Sometimes a person will instinctively protect himself/herself against dealing with that pain by going through some maneuvers which in technical terms are called "resistance." You may or may not be aware of *what* you are avoiding. You may or may not be aware of the *ways* in which you are avoiding it. They could include talking about irrelevant things in the therapy sessions, missing appointments, suddenly deciding that you don't have time for therapy and/or that you can't afford it, feelings of boredom, disappointment, or confusion, disagreements with the therapist about what direction treatment should take at a particular time, sudden "physical" illnesses, even premature termination of therapy. The resistance could extend over a period of time or could be restricted to just one issue; it might even come up in just one session.

Resistance, then, is a way of avoiding emotional pain, and it is normal for people to want to avoid pain. Normal—but not always useful. In a therapy situation it is necessary to go ahead and deal with it. Overcoming resistance is a positive sign of growth, and working through the resistance is usually less painful than maintaining it. If an atmosphere of basic, proven trust has been established and forms a solid basis for the therapy relationship, the client/patient will usually find the courage, strength, and support to overcome the resistance.

A MATCH THAT IS NO LONGER PRODUCTIVE

A bad therapist–client/patient match would be an obvious obstacle to productive therapy. In Chapter 5 we explored some of the elements that go into making a good match when entering therapy and suggested that if the prospective match seemed to be a bad one, you should terminate the relationship and continue to seek out a better one. The concept of spotting a bad match at the very beginning is easy enough to understand. A little more difficult to grasp is that what was once a good match may become a nonproductive relationship later on. For example, you may do some good and productive work with one therapist, then reach a point where the therapist has given you everything he/she can in terms of your personal issues, even though you still have some unresolved problems.

WHAT TO DO

If you have doubts, complaints, or dissatisfaction concerning a therapist, the course of treatment, or anything else, the first course of action is—*discuss it with your therapist.* "If the differences cannot be ironed out between the two of you (or the group if it is a case of group therapy), then you are faced with the choice of getting another opinion or terminating therapy [with that therapist]. A therapist should not be insulted if you ask for a consultation. . . . Seeking

96

another opinion is not an irrevocable step away from your therapist. [In fact,] the therapist may benefit from the insights provided by another [therapist] as much as you will" (*Maze,* p. 47). We recommend that the third party in the consultation be a therapist who is mutually agreed on by both you and your therapist.

"If the diagnosis or prognosis which was given at the time of the evaluation changes drastically and/or you do not understand what the therapist means, those are [two] good reasons to seek a second opinion. In contrast, one or two unsatisfactory or discouraging sessions probably do not indicate the need to look elsewhere. You or the therapist may have an "off" day, or you may have reached a plateau or a difficult place in therapy. Sometimes the difference between being frustrated with the therapy and being frustrated by your own emotional problems is a difficult on-the-spot judgment to make. Likewise, [it is difficult to tell] the difference between disliking the therapist and disliking the discomfort that psychotherapy sometimes brings. If you are in doubt, consult first with your own therapist. If you are unsatisfied with his/her response and remain unhappy with the results of therapy, then consult [with another therapist]. Having once established, after the evaluation period, that you have made a good 'match,' if you suddenly want to terminate therapy for negative reasons (e.g., dissatisfaction with your therapist as opposed to attainment of selected goals), then you might want a second opinion" (*Maze*, p. 47).

"On the other hand, if you repeatedly feel frustrated by therapy or think that the [therapist] consistently does not understand your point of view, consider terminating therapy [with that therapist]" (*Maze*, p. 48). Look for another therapist with whom you can work.

"Although the work of therapy can be painful and difficult, in general a sense of progress, improvement, comfort, etc., should prevail over distress and pain. In other words, the client/patient who complains of lack of progress but continues with the therapist is partly responsible for the dilemma. In cases where the therapist makes recommendations in a direction counter to the inclination of the patient, and a stand-off results, an independent consultant should be brought into the case" (*Maze*, p. 48).

UNETHICAL THERAPIST

One final obstacle to therapy needs to be dealt with—unethical behavior by the therapist.

Unethical financial behavior would include borrowing money from the client/patient, overcharging, charging both the individual and the insurance company, and not telling the client/patient how much the insurance company has paid where the company does not report the amount directly to the individual.

In the sexual area, any action or demand on the part of the therapist that violates standard concepts of morality should be challenged directly. Any sexually suggestive physical contact or any erogenous stroking between the therapist and the client/patient is strictly out of line. There is no place for overt sexual activity in a psychotherapy relationship.

A breach of confidentiality—for example, a therapist releasing your records to anyone without your consent—would also be considered unethical.

"If you feel that some real abuse of good faith or [unethical action] has taken place, you rightfully should take some sort of action" (*Maze* p. 48). You can contact your local mental health association for the name of the appropriate professional group where you can file a complaint. Local or state licensing or certification bureaus should also be informed of any unethical procedure.

"If you do not feel that your rights are defended adequately by any of [these] actions . . . you can consult an attorney for possible alternative remedies. Complaining to the appropriate body or consulting a lawyer are both serious actions, unwarranted for minor differences. . . . You will [probably] be able to work out such differences without resorting to such strong action. [But] strong remedies are available and appropriate if real abuse exists" (*Maze,* p. 49).

99

11

What Do I Do when I Am Finished?

HOW TO TERMINATE THERAPY

You and your therapist have examined the goals
you set for therapy—those you had when you began
and the revised or restated goals you set as a result of
the changes which occurred during the therapeutic
process—and both of you have agreed it is time to
terminate therapy, that you are ready to "go it alone."
In long-term therapy (and often in short-term
therapy), you and your therapist have built a strong
relationship, one you've probably come to depend on.
In long-term therapy there is often a feeling of hostility in "letting go," even when you recognize that
therapy is over. If this happens, it is best to work
through these feelings with your therapist. They are
very appropriate feelings—loss, anger, sadness—so
allow yourself to experience them and to express
them to your therapist. You can process the expecta-
tions of how you will feel when the therapeutic relationship ends prior to termination. Even so, most of
the time the feelings become more intense *after* the

actual termination. If the feelings are so intense as to be debilitating, it would be wise to contact your therapist. You may have left therapy prematurely.

Even when termination was not premature—when the judgment of you and your therapist was correct about your contract being completed—some months or years later a situation may arise in which it would be appropriate to make a new contract, perhaps even with a new therapist. Life is a process in which there is change and crisis. To go back into therapy is not a sign of failure but rather a legitimate use of your new skills in recognizing when additional therapy would be appropriate and helpful. There may also be situations you must deal with that are painful but don't require therapy. The skills you have acquired should help in distinguishing one from the other. In any case, you should always feel free to go back and consult with your therapist if you wish to do so, even for a single interview.

In considering termination, you may have concern about how to replace the close, open relationships that you found with your therapist or your therapy group. It will be very useful for you to consider this need as part of your preparation for termination before therapy is over.

WAYS TO CONTINUE TO GROW

Termination is the time to use the self-knowledge

104

and inner strength you've gained in therapy to reach out and expand your own life in a manner that suits you. Each of us is an individual and our values are different, so there are no all-purpose guidelines about how to achieve this growth. One way to continue to grow and learn is to utilize community programs as mentioned in Chapter 2. You have probably already become aware that you are perceiving others differently and that they are responding to you differently. This is a natural and expected part of your growth. You may wish to invest in closer, more intimate relationships. Or you may choose to limit closer relationships but expand your circle of acquaintances to include more people without feeling you must become deeply involved with each of them. You may wish to use the energy you find you now have in ways you wouldn't have attempted prior to therapy. You may discover that now you can do some of the things that earlier you had only dreamed of doing, because now you have the tools for expressing yourself in ways you hadn't realized before. Growth is now up to you.

Your therapy is finished. You have reached your therapeutic goals. You may feel a sense of loss, but have with it the realization that your new beginning is a reality—and already under way.

12

But This Is an Emergency!

Each person's definition of "emergency" is the one which counts. If you feel yourself to be in an emergency situation, you can:

1. "Call the police if a threat to life, limb, or property exists" (*Maze,* p. 3). They will detain an individual and help determine the alternatives for care. Where there is a local mental health center, the center is frequently consulted directly by the police. Transportation may be arranged by the police or emergency vehicle if necessary.

2. Call your local emergency medical services unit or an ambulance if a person appears seriously ill or unconscious from an overdose, suicidal act, alcohol, drugs, etc. Get the person to a hospital emergency room where he or she can be treated and additional care arranged.

3. Anyone who suddenly becomes disoriented in time or place, or exhibits unusually bizarre behavior needs medical attention immediately. When these symptoms appear in someone of advanced age, they should not be ignored. Whatever a person's age, some physical illnesses and some drugs can cause behav-

ioral symptoms of severe mental illness. If medical attention is received without delay, treatment can often be successful.

4. In communities with mental health centers, the centers often have their own emergency services.

We recommend that you familiarize yourself with the emergency facilities in your community and their telephone numbers before an emergency arises.

SUGGESTED READINGS

Adams, Sallie, and Orgel, Michael. *Through the Mental Health Maze.*
> (Two sections. The first is the main text; the second is a guide to therapists in Washington, D.C.) Available from Health Research Group, Room 708, 2000 P Street, N.W., Washington, D.C. 20036, for $4.00 (both parts).

Bellak, Leopold, and Small, Leonard. *Emergency Psychotherapy and Brief Psychotherapy.* New York: Grune & Stratton, 1965.

"Choosing a Psychotherapist Who's Right for You," *Today's Health* 52(1974):62.

Coudert, Jo. *Advice from a Failure.* New York: Stein & Day, 1965.

Fitts, William H. *Experience of Psychotherapy: What It's Like for Client and Therapist.* New York: Van Nostrand Reinhold, 1965.

Gottman, J., and Leiblum, S. *Psychotherapy and How to Evaluate It: A Manual for Beginners.* New York: Holt, Reinhart & Winston, 1974.

Horn, J. "Guide to Finding the Right Therapist: Through the Mental Health Maze," *Psychology Today* 9(1976):95-96.

Kiernan, Thomas P. *Shrinks, etc.: A Consumer's Guide to Psychotherapies.* New York: Dial, 1974.

Liss, Jerome. *Free to Feel.* New York: Praeger, 1974.

Park, Clara C., and Shapiro, Leon. *You Are Not Alone!*

Understanding and Dealing with Mental Illness. Boston: Little, Brown, 1976.

Shapiro, Stephen, and Tyrka, Hilary. *Trusting Yourself: Psychotherapy as a Beginning.* Englewood Cliffs, N. J.: Prentice-Hall, 1975.

Stuart, Richard B. *Trick and Treatment: How and When Psychotherapy Fails.* Champaign, Ill.: Research Press, 1970.

Walkenstein, Eileen. *Beyond the Couch.* New York: Crown, 1972.